FOX
Curious Kids Press

Thanks for checking out the Curious Kids Press Series. Please note: All Rights Reserved. No part of this publication may be reproduced in any form or by any means, including scanning, photocopying, or otherwise without prior written permission of the copyright holder. Copyright © 2013

Foxes

Have you ever heard of a "clever fox?" Foxes are extremely smart animals and can be found all over the world. They are members of the dog family, and though they look very cute with their bushy tails and fluffy fur, they are wild animals! There are so many different kinds of foxes, and all of them have traits that make them special and unique. Would you like to learn more about foxes? Keep reading!

Where Foxes Live

Foxes can live in so many different kinds of habitats! They can be found in forests, woodlands, deserts, mountains, and near the ocean. Some foxes even live in the warm tropics and icy arctic regions! Foxes can be found in North America, South America, Europe, Australia, and parts of Asia.

Fox Homes

Foxes make their homes in many places. Some foxes sleep in small caves or under rocks. Other foxes like to live in hollow logs or under bushes. Arctic foxes dig deep holes in the snow. Many foxes like to burrow into the ground. A fox's home is called a den.

What Foxes Look Like

Foxes belong to the dog family, even though they are wild animals! They have pointed noses and ears shaped like triangles. Their bodies are covered in thick, long fur that can be red, yellow, brown, gray, white or black. A fox's fluffy tail is almost as long as it's body!

Baby Foxes

Foxes give birth to live babies that are called kits, pups, or cubs. Foxes can have litters of four to eleven babies at a time! Baby foxes drink milk from their mothers until they are old enough to eat other foods. When they get older, they are playful like puppies!

Adult Foxes

Adult male foxes are called dogs. Adult females are called vixens. Females usually give birth to one litter each year, and both parents help to take care of the babies. Foxes will mark the area they live and hunt in with their scent. Foxes usually live for about 10 years.

A Fox's Senses

Foxes are known to be very clever animals. They have excellent senses of hearing, sight, and smell. Foxes are even able to see well in the dark! Foxes can hear other animals from very far away. Foxes also have their own special stinky odor, which helps keep bigger predators away.

What Foxes Eat

Foxes are omnivores. Omnivores are animals that like to eat both meat and plants. Foxes are excellent hunters and catch small animals like birds, chipmunks, and mice. They will also eat fruits, grains, and vegetables. Foxes will even eat insects and bird's eggs! Some foxes will even eat dead animals.

Foxes and People

Some people, like farmers, do not like foxes because they can kill animals like chickens. Others find them useful, because they keep mice and other rodents away. Sometimes people hunt foxes for their beautiful fur. People have even tried to keep foxes as pets even though they are wild animals.

Endangered Foxes

Some foxes are endangered, which means that there are only a few remaining in the wild. The arctic fox is endangered because it is hunted for its beautiful white fur. Hunting, pollution, and destruction of the places an animal lives are all things that can cause it to become endangered.

Red Foxes

Red foxes can be found all over the world. Red foxes usually have reddish fur and white tipped tails. Red foxes can live in a variety of places, including woodlands and deserts. Red foxes can even be found in cities and towns. They eat mice, rabbits, and other small creatures.

Arctic Foxes

Arctic foxes live where it is very cold. They dig deep burrows into the snow, and have long fur to keep them warm. Some Arctic foxes have white fur. Other Arctic foxes have bluish gray fur. They hunt rabbits and other small animals. Arctic foxes are an endangered species.

Fennec Foxes

Fennec foxes are the smallest foxes. They live in North Africa and Saudi Arabia. They have extra hair on their feet to protect them from the hot desert sand. Fennec foxes hunt small animals like lizards and insects. They find water by digging up and eating the roots of plants.

Gray Foxes

Gray foxes are found in Canada, Mexico, and the United States. The gray fox has shorter fur that is gray on top and reddish underneath. It has smaller ears than most foxes. The gray fox has a unique and special ability. It is the only fox that can climb trees!

Kit Foxes

Kit foxes live in North America. Kit foxes have fur that is gray, yellow, and white. There are many kinds of kit foxes. The swift fox is the fastest fox and can run 25 miles per hour. The desert kit fox has large ears that help to keep it cool.

Bat Eared Fox

The bat eared fox has large, triangle shaped ears that stick out from its head, similar to the way a bat's wings stick out. These ears help to keep it cool, as it lives in very hot parts of Africa. Bat eared foxes eat insects, fruit, and some small animals.

Pale Fox

The pale fox is a rare fox that lives in the Sahara desert. It is a very small fox with large ears and light fur that blends into the sand. It eats fruit and animals. It can hold water like a camel, and does not have to drink very often.

Darwin's Fox

Darwin's foxes live in the country of Chile in South America. It is one of the smallest foxes, with a short tail and black and gray fur. These foxes live in deeply wooded forests. Darwin's fox is endangered, and there are only around 300 of them left in the world.

Cape Fox

The cape fox lives in the open grasslands of southern Africa. They have a loud bark, and communicate with soft chirps and whines. They are nocturnal, which means that they are awake at night. Cape foxes are small and often hunted by owls, hawks, and large cats such as leopards.

Bengal Fox

The Bengal fox is also called the Indian fox, because it lives in India. They make a noise that sounds like a chattering cry, and will also growl, whine, or bark. They spend half of the day in their burrows before going out to hunt reptiles, birds, and small rodents.

Island Fox

The island fox can only be found on a small group of islands near the coast of California. They hunt birds, reptiles, crabs, and other small animals. Island foxes are hunted by golden eagles, so they try to stay under bushes and trees where they won't be seen from the sky!

Thank you for checking out another addition from Curious Kids Press! Make sure to search "Curious Kids Press" on Amazon.com for many other great titles.

Printed in the USA
CPSIA information can be obtained
at www.ICGtesting.com
LVHW061111251123
764786LV00016B/3